LOOK INSIDE

A SHAKESPEAREAN THEATRE

PETER CHRISP
Illustrated by Adam Hook

Editor: Jason Hook
Designer: Jean Wheeler
Cover Designer: Rachel Hamdi
Picture Research: Shelley Noronha

First published in Great Britain in 1998 by
Wayland (Publishers) Ltd
Reprinted in 2000 by Hodder Wayland,
an imprint of Hodder Children's Books

This edition published in 2007 by Wayland,
an imprint of Hachette Children's Books
Reprinted in 2008

A catalogue record for this book is available from the
British Library

ISBN 978 0 7502 5210 2

Printed and bound in China

Hachette Children's Books
338 Euston Road, London NW1 3BH

Picture Acknowledgements: The publishers would like to
thank the following for permission to publish their pictures:
(t=top; c=centre; b=bottom; l=left; r=right) AKG London
/Musee du Louvre 6t, /Bibliotheque Nationale, Paris 26b; Andy
Chopping, Museum of London Archaeology Service © MoL 9t,
9br, 10b; Ashmolean Museum, Oxford 20t; Bridgeman Art
Library, London/New York, /British Library cover (c), 28b,
/Edinburgh University Library 7t, /Fitzwilliam Museum,
University of Cambridge 8b, /Dulwich Picture Gallery 14t, 15t,
/Victoria and Albert Museum 20cl; Bruce Coleman, /Dr Sandro
Prato 11t; Christie's Images 12tl; © The Board of Trustees of
the Armouries, TR.354 22t; Corpus Christi College,
Cambridge 16b; Edinburgh University Library 7b, 10t; E.T.
Archive 6b, 8t, 21b, 26t, 27t; Fine Art Photographic Library
5t; Folger Shakespeare Library 9bl, 23t; Fotomas Index 16t,
18b, 19t, 25t, 28t; Glasgow Museums cover (br), 21t; Mary
Rose Trust cover (tr), 11c, 15bl; Museum of London border
corners, 13br, 17t, 20br, 29t, /Walter Hodges 4b; National
Portrait Gallery 17b, 23b, 27b; National Trust Photographic
Library /John Hammond 12t; Oxford Scientific Films cover
(bl), 24t; Scottish National Portrait Gallery 24b; Shakespeare's
Globe /Richard Kalina 4t, 13tr, 19cr, /John Tramper 14b,
15br, 22b; Wayland Picture Library 11b, 19b, /Richard Hook
6c; Weiss Gallery 12b.

All quotes are credited on page 31.

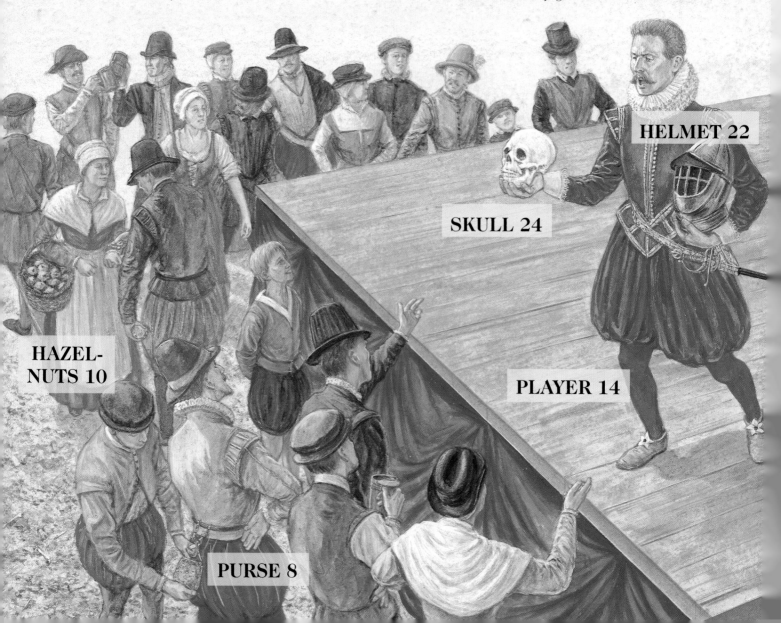

HELMET 22

SKULL 24

HAZEL-
NUTS 10

PLAYER 14

PURSE 8

CONTENTS

The Tragicall History of the Life and Death of Doctor Faustus

▲ Shakespeare's theatre, called the Globe, has been rebuilt close to its original site.

THE PLAYHOUSE

Look inside a theatre in the time of William Shakespeare. You enter through a small doorway, and find yourself in a crowded, noisy yard, open to the sky. A large stage sticks out in front of you. Around the sides, there are covered galleries full of richly dressed men and women. This is one of the most famous sights in London. Every visitor to the city tries to go to a playhouse, as theatres are called.

'Playhouses are the meeting places for beggars, thieves, horse-stealers [and] plotters of treason. They draw apprentices and other servants away from their work and all sorts of people from Christian worship.' [2]

▼ The Rose Theatre in London.

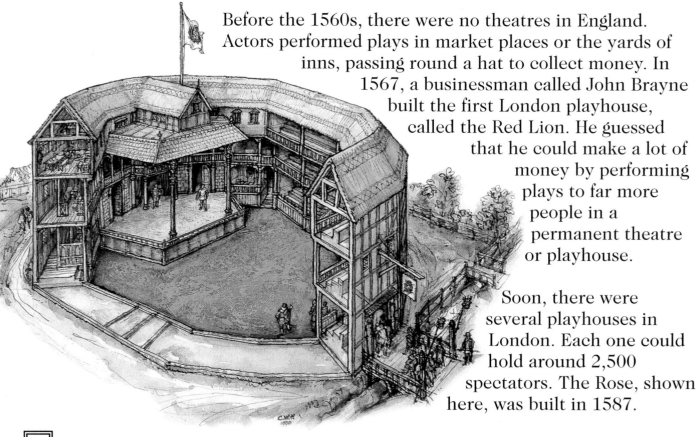

Before the 1560s, there were no theatres in England. Actors performed plays in market places or the yards of inns, passing round a hat to collect money. In 1567, a businessman called John Brayne built the first London playhouse, called the Red Lion. He guessed that he could make a lot of money by performing plays to far more people in a permanent theatre or playhouse.

Soon, there were several playhouses in London. Each one could hold around 2,500 spectators. The Rose, shown here, was built in 1587.

The playhouses were built just outside the city, away from the power of the Lord Mayor and the aldermen, the rich men who governed London. They hated playhouses, and did everything they could to get the theatres closed down.

TRAVELS IN ENGLAND
by three German gentlemen

Outside the city are some theatres, where actors play almost every day to crowds of people. 1

▲ You can find out more information about all quotes and where they come from, by looking on page 31.

◀ Most playhouses were at Bankside, on the south of the River Thames.

◀ A thatcher works on the roof of the Globe, which was built in 1598-9.

TRUMPET

WATERMEN AND CHURCH BELLS

A trumpeter climbs up on to the balcony, high above the stage. He blows three loud blasts. At the sound of the trumpet, latecomers hurry inside the playhouse. The noisy audience falls silent, and all eyes turn to the stage. Everyone knows that the play is about to start.

▲ A loud trumpet-blast was the best way to grab the audience's attention.

On a day when a play was to be performed, a brightly coloured silk flag was flown above the theatre. The flag had a picture on it showing the name of the playhouse, such as a globe, a rose or a swan. Picture signs were important, because few people could read.

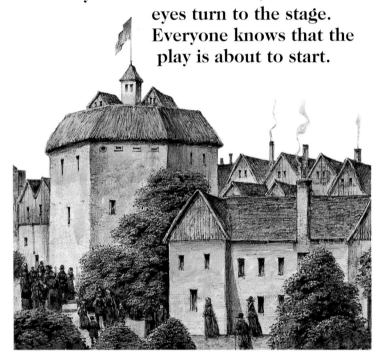

▲ The audience arrives at the Globe.

▼ The playhouse flags could be seen across the river from the city, where most of the audience lived and worked.

There was only one bridge across the Thames, London Bridge. Most people crossed the river by boat, hiring 'watermen' who were the taxi drivers of the day. Playhouses were a wonderful new source of business for them. By 1614, watermen and their families living by the river numbered 40,000.

◀ Watermen row a party of rich passengers across the Thames.

The loudest sound heard in London was the ringing of church bells. There were more than a hundred churches in the city, and you can see their towers in the picture at the bottom of page 6. The church bells rang out to call the Londoners to Christian worship.

▼ Some members of the audience crossed London Bridge on horseback.

'Will not a filthy play, with the blast of a trumpet, sooner call thither [attract] a thousand, than an hour's tolling of a bell bring to the sermon a hundred?' 3

PURSE

CUTPURSES

At the theatre entrance, each member of the audience hands over a silver penny, the price of entry to the yard. They are watched by a man leaning against the wall. He is a cutpurse, a thief looking for a likely victim. Soon he will take advantage of the jostling crowd, and make his move.

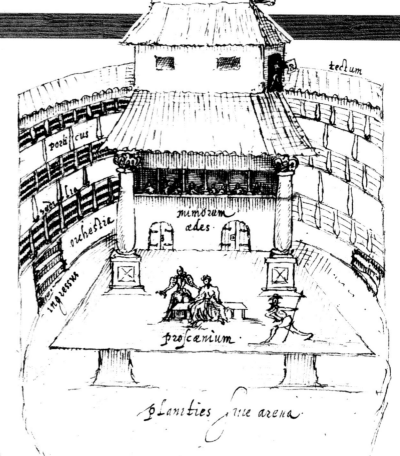

▶ The Swan playhouse, drawn in 1596. It cost extra to sit in the raised galleries.

Most clothes did not have pockets, so people carried their money in purses attached to their clothes by a drawstring. A cutpurse would cut the string to take the purse, or cut a hole in the purse to get at the money.

'And here and there, a cutpurse thrusts and leers, with hawks' eyes for his prey.' [4]

◀ A richly embroidered purse.

Wherever there was a crowd, you found cutpurses. A packed playhouse was the perfect place for them. People were so busy watching the action on the stage, that they did not notice the cutpurse standing next to them.

'Every year, more than three hundred thieves are hanged in London.' [5]

▶ These coins were found at the Rose playhouse.

Cutpurses were sometimes caught in the act of stealing. They were dragged up onto the stage, tied to one of the wooden posts, and pelted with rubbish.

▶ John Selman, a cutpurse, was hanged in 1612.

'Somebody once picked a pocket in this playhouse yard, was hoisted onto the stage and shamed about it.' [6]

The easiest place to take purses was in the crowded yard. However, it was more profitable to steal from the rich people in the galleries. Some cutpurses, such as John Selman, dressed as gentlemen in order to mingle with the rich. He was hanged for stealing a purse during a royal performance.

▶ Some people carried pennies in pottery money-jars, like these ones found at the Rose.

HAZELNUTS

THE PENNY STINKARDS

In the yard in front of the stage, the poorest members of the audience drink ale. Some hiss loudly to show their boredom. Others throw apples at the players. Some go to the toilet where they stand! The ground is covered with hazelnut shells to soak up their mess. It smells awful.

▲ A poor farmer, up from the countryside to see a play.

All sorts of people stood in the crowded yard. There were fish porters, farm workers, soldiers, sailors, butchers, shoemakers and servants. The only thing they had in common was that everyone else looked down on them. They were nicknamed 'groundlings', 'penny stinkards' and 'scarecrows'.

◀ A woman stinkard hurls an apple at the players.

'The stinkards oft will hiss without a cause,
And for a bawdy jest will give applause.
Let one but ask the reason why they roar.
They'll answer, 'cause the rest did so before.' [7]

◀ Archaeologists found that the yards at the Rose and the Globe theatres had floors of hazelnut shells, cinders and sand.

The groundlings were nicknamed 'stinkards' because they liked to chew raw garlic. A number of actors complained that you could smell the foul breath of the stinkards up on the stage.

▲ Cloves of garlic for the stinkards.

In these theatres, fruits such as apples, pears and nuts are carried about to be sold, as well as wine and ale.

The worst behaved groundlings were the apprentices – boys and young men learning trades in the city. Sometimes, these rowdy apprentices rioted at the theatres. In 1617, a mob of apprentices went on the rampage at the Cockpit playhouse. They wounded several actors and wrecked the theatre.

◀ A wooden tankard. As the groundlings got drunk on ale, fights often broke out.

Women called 'apple-wives' walked around the playhouse yard, carrying baskets of apples for sale. Everyone in the audience liked apples. Nobles bought them to offer to the ladies, and the groundlings liked to hurl them at the actors.

▲ Apples were popular both as missiles and for food.

'We may be pelted off for ought we know, With apples, eggs, or stones, from thence below.' [8]

CUSHION

LADIES AND GALLANTS

In the gallery, a young gallant bows to a lady and waves his handkerchief. He is richly dressed, with a huge white ruff around his neck and a dark blue velvet suit, decorated with pearls. 'How do you, pretty lady!' says the gallant, 'May I offer you this cushion?' She takes the cushion gratefully, and settles down to watch the play.

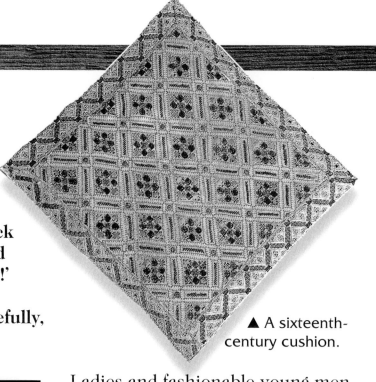

▲ A sixteenth-century cushion.

Ladies and fashionable young men called gallants, spent a lot of money on the latest fashions. When they went to the theatre, they wanted people to look at them and admire their clothes. Some sat in the balcony at the back of the stage. They did not care that the players had their backs to them. It was more important to be the centre of attention.

Sometimes gallants paid extra to sit on a stool on the stage itself. This was the best place to show off your fine clothes and elegant legs, while making loud comments about the play. The only risk was that the stinkards might make fun of you.

▲ Rich people liked to show off their fashionable and elaborate clothes.

'Though the stinkards in the yard hoot at you, hiss at you, yea throw dirt even in your teeth, 'tis most gentlemanlike patience to endure all this and to laugh at the silly animals.' [9]

'You shall see such heaving and shoving to sit by women, such pillows to their backs, that they take no hurt, such giving them pippins to pass the time.' [10]

If a man desires to sit on a cushion in the most comfortable place of all, where he not only sees everything well, but can also be seen, then he gives yet another English penny at another door.

▲ Oak stools for sitting on the stage.

A play written in 1604 called *The Malcontent* begins with the player William Sly coming on stage dressed as a gallant, and sitting on a stool. Warned by a stagehand not to sit there, he replies: 'Why? Dost think I fear hissing? I'll hold my life thou tookest me for one of the players! Let them that have stale suits sit in the galleries.'

▶ In the 1590s, the latest fashion for a gallant was a watch, worn around the neck on a chain.

◀ A young gallant buys a pippin from the apple-wife.

13

PLAYER

SHARERS AND HIRED MEN

The actor Nathan Field sits quite still, his right hand resting on his breast. He is having his portrait painted. 'You players have done very well for yourselves,' says the artist. 'A few years ago, I would never have been asked to paint a player's portrait!'

▲ Nathan Field, was a star at the Globe. He played the lead roles in romantic plays.

The actors or 'players' belonged to companies, each named after a rich nobleman or lady. These nobles were the actors' protectors. Shakespeare's company was called the Lord Chamberlain's Men, later the King's Men. It was illegal to perform plays without a noble's licence. Actors who did so could be whipped and branded.

There were different types of player in a company. The most important were called 'sharers'. They paid the theatre expenses, and shared the profits. Below them were the 'hired men', who were paid by the week. There were also apprentice players – boys learning to be actors, who played all the women's roles until their voices broke.

◄ Players used many different hand gestures as part of their performance.

▲ William Sly often played the role of a fashionable gallant.

Two men in men's clothes and two men in women's clothes gave this performance, in wonderful combination with each other.

▶ This richly dressed actor is playing a French knight in *Henry V.*

Like today, actors became famous for playing certain types of role. William Sly, a skilled swordsman, was given lots of action scenes. Nathan Field played young lovers, and had many women fans. The biggest star of all was Richard Burbage, who played kings in history plays and heroes in tragedies.

It was thirsty work acting on stage for two hours or more. The players got through plenty of ale between scenes. They drank from pewter tankards, like the one shown here.

◀ A sixteenth-century tankard.

PLAYBOOK

PLAYS AND PLAYWRIGHTS

'**W**ho will buy a playbook?' shouts the bookseller, walking around the upper gallery. He carries a basket full of small paper-bound books. 'Look sirs, *Doctor Faustus*, lately performed in this very playhouse.' He holds up a copy, showing the title page. 'Do you remember when the devil appeared? Here's a picture of the scene, and only sixpence.'

The Tragicall History of the Life and Death of *Doctor Faustus*.

Written by *Ch. Marklin*.

LONDON,
Printed for *Iohn Wright*, and are to be fold at his fhop
without Newgate, at the ſ....ſ the
Bib: 1616.

▶ The title page of *Doctor Faustus*, by Christopher Marlowe.

'*Oh, thou art fairer than the evening's air,
Clad in the beauty of a thousand stars.*' [11]
Doctor Faustus

Playwrights were called poets, because serious plays were always written in verse. From 1587 to 1593, the leading poet was Christopher Marlowe. He gave the actors at the Rose Theatre wonderful verse to speak, with lines that could make the audience's hairs stand up on end.

◀ The playwright Christopher Marlowe. He was stabbed to death at the age of 29.

◀ People loved poetry. Some ate from 'trenchers' like these, decorated with verse.

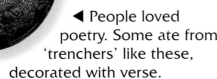

In these plays, the English learn what is going on in other lands.

For the most part, the English do not travel. They prefer to learn of foreign matters at home.

Plays were written to be performed, not read. Usually, the sharers who ran the companies did not want to publish them. Sharers like William Shakespeare wanted to stop rival companies getting hold of their plays. But some plays were published, usually by hired actors hoping to make a little extra money.

If a play at one theatre was a big hit, all the London poets would write similar types of play. In the early 1600s, there was a craze for 'revenge plays'. These were tragedies showing a murder, which is then avenged with lots of bloodshed. They were usually set abroad – the audience preferred to see foreigners doing wicked things!

◀ William Shakespeare wrote the most famous revenge play of all, called *Hamlet*.

'So shall you hear
Of carnal, bloody and unnatural acts,
Of accidental judgments,
casual slaughters.'[12] Hamlet

TRAPDOOR

SPECIAL EFFECTS

Beneath the stage, the waiting stagehand hears an actor's loud rapping above his head. At this signal, he quickly pulls open the trapdoor. He plays a drum-roll as an actor, clutching a firework and dressed as a devil, jumps up through the trapdoor. He appears on stage in a cloud of smoke.

'One may behold shaggy-haired devils run roaring over the stage with squibs [fireworks] in their mouths, while drummers make thunder.' [13]

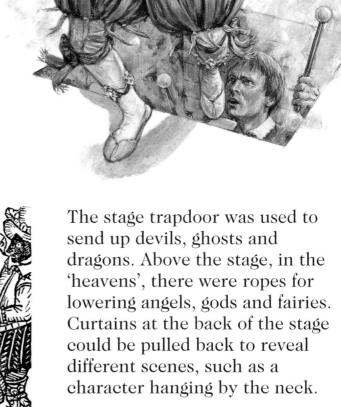

▶ A devil leaps from the area under the stage known as 'hell', while a stagehand beats a drum.

▲ In *The Spanish Tragedy*, a wooden frame supports an actor to make it look like he has been hanged.

The stage trapdoor was used to send up devils, ghosts and dragons. Above the stage, in the 'heavens', there were ropes for lowering angels, gods and fairies. Curtains at the back of the stage could be pulled back to reveal different scenes, such as a character hanging by the neck.

Stage direction: 'Merlin strikes his wand. Thunder and lightning. Two dragons appear, a white and a red.' [14]

Props were used to create different special effects. The Rose playhouse had something called a 'frame for the heading', which was used in beheading scenes.

Finally, a rocket was shot into a rosette which hung above. From this rosette, apples and pears fell onto the people standing below ...

The show ended with rockets and fireworks flying from all corners.

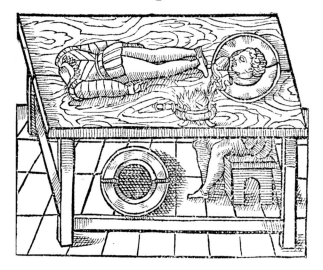

▲ A trick table, to give the effect of a head cut from a body.

The stage was usually bare. It could stand for any place – the deck of a ship, a forest or a desert. The two pillars on the stage could represent trees or a ship's masts. The doors at the back might be the gates of a city.

▼ You can see the two pillars on the stage at the rebuilt Globe.

No special lighting was used, for plays were put on in daylight. Everything depended on what the actors did and said. The audience was expected to use its imagination. When the actors shivered and talked about the wind and rain, the people in the crowd believed a storm was raging.

◄ An actor carrying a candle let the audience know it was night.

'Let us ... on your imaginary forces work ...
Think when we talk of horses that you see them ...
For 'tis your thoughts that now must
deck [dress] our kings.' 15

GLOVES

COSTUMES

Behind the stage lies the 'tiring-house', or dressing room. Here the boy actors who play women are quickly pulling on their wigs, their silk, satin and velvet dresses, and their embroidered gloves. The audience expects to see players in magnificent costumes. Some are more interested in staring at the costumes than listening to the play!

▲ An ornate pair of gloves.

A playwright listed people's reasons for going to the playhouse:
'Some in wit, some in shows
Take delight, and some in clothes.' [16]

▲ Costumes used in a masque in 1589.

Sometimes, the players were asked to put on a special performance for the royal court, called a masque. At a masque, the nobles and the players all wore specially designed, gorgeous costumes. If the players were lucky, they could keep their costumes to use in the theatre later.

▲ A leather jacket or 'jerkin' made in 1558.

Different classes in society were expected to dress differently. It was against the law to dress 'above your station'. You could be locked up or fined for wearing material that was too expensive or colourful.

◄ Only nobles and actors could wear such a beautiful jacket.

Players were the only people able to get away with dressing above their station. This was because they had the protection of royalty and the nobles, who loved watching plays.

Some plays, such as Shakespeare's *Titus Andronicus*, were set in ancient Rome. People knew Romans dressed differently from themselves, but they were not sure how. So, players performed in dress of their own time, adding the odd robe as a 'Roman' touch.

▼ *Titus Andronicus*, drawn by a spectator at the Rose in 1595.

HELMET

BATTLES AND POLITICS

'**O**n, on you noble English!' shouts Richard Burbage, who is playing King Henry V. In gleaming helmets and armour, the players charge across the stage. Trumpets blast, a cannon is fired, and the audience cheers loudly. Above the noise, King Henry yells out the battle-cry: 'God for Harry! England and St George!'

▲ Helmets like this were worn for battle scenes.

◀ Actors at the modern Globe, dressed for Shakespeare's *Henry V.*

From 1585 to 1604, England was at war with Spain. The long war gave people a taste for history plays with battle scenes. Visitors to the Globe could watch plays showing King Henry V and John Talbot, a famous general, invading France. The audience loved seeing English heroes beating foreigners.

'How it would have joyed brave Talbot, the terror of the French, to think that after he had lain two hundred years in his tomb, he should triumph again on the stage.' 17

Theatre was the most popular entertainment in London. But the Lord Mayor and his aldermen believed crowded theatres were a threat to law and order. They often asked Queen Elizabeth for permission to close down the playhouses.

The English are powerful in war, successful against their enemies, and vastly fond of loud noises that fill the ear, such as the firing of cannon, drums, and the ringing of bells. If they see a handsome and well-built foreigner, they will say, 'It is a pity he is not an Englishman.'

◀ A London alderman in 1598.

In 1602, the aldermen needed to find soldiers to fight in the war. They sent 'press-gangs' to the playhouses, and rounded up 4,500 men. The aldermen expected to find only poor commoners at the plays. They were embarrassed to learn that they had press-ganged several lawyers and noblemen, including an earl.

'All old plays ought to be brought to the Master of Revels, since they may be full of offensive things against Church and State.' [18]

Queen Elizabeth had an official called the Master of Revels, who read every play before it was allowed to be performed. He cut out bad language, as well as any scenes showing disrespect to kings, queens or the Church.

▶ Queen Elizabeth I liked plays, but she preferred to watch bear-baiting.

SKULL

BLOOD AND BRAWLS

The star actor Nathan Field walks slowly down to the front of the stage. In one hand, he holds up a human skull, which he gazes at with a look of horror. 'Thou shell of death!' he cries, 'Once the bright face of my betrothed lady!'

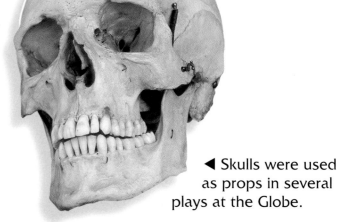

◀ Skulls were used as props in several plays at the Globe.

▲ Mary Queen of Scots was executed in 1587 in front of an audience.

Stage direction: 'He thrusts out his head, and they cut off a false head made of a bladder filled with blood.' [19]

Theatre audiences loved the sight of blood. People watched public executions for entertainment, and the heads of those executed were stuck on spikes over London Bridge. Several plays had gruesome execution scenes. In *The Battle of Alcazar*, three characters were 'disembowelled'. The audience gasped as the bloody liver, heart and lungs of a sheep were pulled out of each actor's false stomach.

People enjoyed watching cruel blood sports, such as fights between bears and dogs. Crowds went to the Bear Garden, near the Globe, to enjoy the whipping of an old, blind bear called Harry Hunks.

▲ A fight scene from a play called *The Maid's Tragedy*.

▼ For fight scenes, actors wore a pig's bladder full of blood, which oozed out when the bladder was pierced by a sword.

Many actors were skilled swordsmen, and used sharp weapons in fight scenes. In 1622, an apprentice standing beside the stage was accidentally cut by an actor's sword. He immediately challenged the actor to a duel.

It was a violent age. Men walked around armed with swords and daggers. The playwrights Christopher Marlowe and Ben Jonson were both involved in sword-fights. Jonson killed fellow actor Gabriel Spencer in a duel. Spencer had himself previously killed a man. Marlowe, after being arrested twice for fighting, was stabbed to death in a tavern.

CLOWN

JIGS AND JESTS

At the end of the show, a clown called Richard Tarlton jumps out onto the stage. The sight of Tarlton's face is enough to get the audience roaring with laughter. He dances across the stage, playing a lively tune on a pipe and drum.

▶ Richard Tarlton was the most famous clown of the 1580s.

▲ A scene from a comedy play performed in the sixteenth century.

Clowns played roles in comedies, and in the comic scenes of tragedies. They annoyed playwrights by making up their own lines, to get more laughs. Tarlton often stopped in the middle of a scene, to insult the stinkards or make fun of the gallants. His jokes were so popular that they were collected in a book called *Tarlton's Jests*.

'Let those that play your clowns speak no more than is set down for them.' [20]

The plays finish with a variety of dances, accompanied by excellent music and the loud applause of everyone present.

'Tarlton when his head was only seen,
The tire-house door and tapestry between,
Set all the multitude in such a laughter,
They could not hold for scarce an
hour after.' 21

In the 1590s, the most popular clown was Will Kemp. He was famous for dancing a jig all the way from London to Norwich. It took Kemp nine days, and large crowds came out to cheer him as he leapt past. He was so proud of his jig that he wrote a book about it, called *Kemp's Nine Days' Wonder*.

▲ Will Kemp dances his way to Norwich.

Will Kemp wrote: 'My taborer [drummer] strikes up and I must to Norwich. Imagine I am now setting off, the hour about seven, the morning gloomy, the company many, my heart merry ... As fast as kind peoples thronging together would give me leave, through London I leapt.' 22

▶ Many plays ended with music and dancing.

TOBACCO, PLAGUE AND FIRE

In the galleries, the gallants light up their pipes and fill the air around them with thick tobacco smoke. Smoking is a new fashion. Some people say that it can protect you from the plague, a terrible disease which can kill thousands of Londoners each summer.

▶ Mary Frith, who shocked people by going to playhouses dressed as a man, and smoking a pipe.

When more than thirty people died from the plague in one week, the playhouses had to close. This happened in 1592 and 1594, when 20,000 Londoners died from the disease. Actors made a living by going on tour instead.

▲ Touring actors perform in a country house.

King James I described smoking as 'a custom loathsome to the eye, hateful to the nose, harmful to the brain, dangerous to the lungs.' [23]

At these shows, and everywhere else, the English are always smoking the nicotine weed called tobacco. They have clay pipes into which they put the herb. Lighting it, they draw the smoke into their mouths, puffing it out again through their nostrils, like funnels, along with plenty of phlegm.

Preachers in London said that God had sent the plague as a punishment for sin. This gave the preachers a chance to complain about the playhouses.

'The cause of plagues is sin, and the cause of sin are plays. Therefore the cause of plagues are plays.' [24]

On 29 June 1613, the Globe was packed with an audience watching Shakespeare's *Henry VIII*. At one point, a cannon was fired as a special effect. Sparks rose through the air and set the thatched roof alight. The flames quickly spread, and within two hours the Globe had burnt to the ground. For the preachers, this was just one more sign of God's anger towards the Shakespearean theatre.

▶ Everyone escaped the fire unhurt, but one man had to put out his burning breeches with beer.

GLOSSARY

aldermen Members of a council, headed by the Lord Mayor, which ruled the city of London.

apprentices Young people being taught a trade.

bawdy Funny and rude.

bear-baiting An entertainment in which a pack of dogs was set on a bear chained to a post.

branded Marked or scarred with a hot iron.

breeches Trousers.

carnal Of the body or flesh.

comedy A light-hearted play with a happy ending.

disembowelled Having the innards removed.

dost An old word meaning 'do' or 'do you'.

gallant A fashionable young man.

gentlemanlike Suitable to a gentleman's good behaviour, gentlemanly.

groundling A member of the theatre audience who paid a penny to stand in the yard.

jerkin A close-fitting, sleeveless jacket.

jest A joke.

jig A dance to the music of a pipe and drum, performed at the end of a play.

loathsome Causing hatred or disgust.

Lord Chamberlain The royal official who gave licences to perform plays.

nobles People belonging to the upper classes.

phlegm The mucous that is brought up by coughing.

pippins Apples.

press-gangs Groups of men who force people to join the army or navy.

rosette A rose-shaped ornament.

ruff A starched frill worn around the neck.

thatcher Someone who makes thatched roofs.

thence An old word meaning 'that place'.

thou An old word meaning 'you'.

tragedy A serious play showing the suffering and death of a great hero or heroine.

treason Illegal acts which threaten your own king or queen.

trenchers Wooden or clay plates.

wit Clever and amusing use of words and ideas.

FURTHER READING

BOOKS TO READ

Shakespeare (Eyewitness Guides) by Peter Chrisp
(Dorling Kindersley, 2004)
A Shakespearean Theatre by Jacqeline Morley
(Book House, 2003)
William Shakespeare (Famous Lives, Famous People)
(Franklin Watts, 2002)
*Shakespeare's Tales- A Midsummer Night's Dream,
Macbeth, Romeo and Juliet, Julius Caesar, Twelfth Night*
and *The Tempest* all by Beverley Birch (Wayland, 2006)

You can visit the Globe Theatre at
Southwark in London. For educational
information, telephone 020 7902 1400

QUOTES

1. The quotations in our book *Travels in England* come from the accounts of three German travellers:
   Lupold von Wedel, *Account of a Visit to England*, 1585
   Paul Hentzner, *Travels in England*, 1598
   Thomas Platter, *Platter's Travels*, 1605

2. The Lord Mayor of London, 28 July 1597.
3. Part of a sermon preached by John Stockwood, a preacher at St Paul's, 1578.
4. From *The Roaring Girl*, a play by John Dekker and Thomas Middleton, 1611.
5. Paul Hentzner, *Travels in England*, 1598.
6. Anonymous, *Nobody and Somebody*, 1606.
7. A description of stinkards copying each other's bad behaviour, from William Fennor, *Fennor's Descriptions*, 1616.
8. Robert Tailor, *The Hog Hath Lost his Pearl*, 1614.
9. The experience of a gallant sitting on stage, from Thomas Dekker, *The Gull's Hornbook*, 1609.
10. A description of the attention paid to women at the theatre, Stephen Gosson, *The School of Abuse*, 1579.
11. Christopher Marlowe, *Doctor Faustus*, 1592.
12. William Shakespeare, *Hamlet*, 1601.
13. John Melton, *Astrologaster*, 1620.
14. William Rowley's play, *The Birth of Merlin*, written in 1608.
15. William Shakespeare, *Henry V*, 1599.
16. Thomas Middleton, *No Wit, No Help Like a Woman's*, 1613.
17. Thomas Nashe, *Pierce Penniless*, 1592.
18. Henry Herbert, Master of Revels, *Diary*, 1633.
19. Stage direction from *The Rebellion of Naples*, 1649.
20. William Shakespeare, *Hamlet*, 1601.
21. Henry Peacham, *Thalia's Banquet*, 1620.
22. Will Kemp, *Kemp's Nine Days' Wonder*, 1600.
23. James I, *A Counterblast to Tobacco*, 1604.
24. Thomas White, A Sermon preached at Paul's Cross, 1578.

INDEX

Numbers in **bold** refer to pictures and captions.